Thérèse of Lisieux

Michael Hollings has been parish priest of St Mary of
the Angels, Bayswater since 1979. He is Chaplain to the
Catholic Institute of International Relations and has
held numerous other chaplaincies, in Westminster,
Oxford and London University. He contributes
regularly to *The Tablet* and has written many books.

MICHAEL HOLLINGS

Thérèse of Lisieux

Photographs by Helmuth Nils Loose

Collins
FOUNT PAPERBACKS

First published in German by Verlag Herder,
Freiburg im Breisgau, 1979, using the text of Jean François Six
Original edition © Verlag Herder, Freiburg im Breisgau, 1979

First published in English by William Collins Sons & Co Ltd, London, 1981
Issued by Fount Paperbacks, London 1982
This edition issued by Fount Paperbacks, London 1984
English text © William Collins Sons & Co Ltd, 1981

The photographer and publishers wish to thank
the following: Mother Marie of the Redemption,
Prioress of the Carmelites of Lisieux; Father
Paul Gires, Director of Pilgrimage of Lisieux;
and M. Gerard Pauc, Central Office of Lisieux

Printed in Great Britain at the University Press, Oxford

Contents

Introduction

The town of Lisieux lies in the rolling wooded folds of Normandy, among the apple orchards. During the advance of the Allies' Second Front attack in 1944, it also lay in the direct path of the breakout from the beachhead through Caen. Caught by bombs and guns, large areas of the town were obliterated, the ancient timbered medieval houses were gutted, and whole streets disappeared. The Allied forces swept through to Paris and beyond. The townsfolk were left to emerge from the rubble, to count their losses and to begin rebuilding.

Three years later, before very much reconstruction had been achieved, I was asked by a well known priest, Monsignor Vernon Johnson, to go with him and another friend to spend some time in Lisieux. Vernon Johnson had been converted to the Roman Catholic Church in the 1920s, because someone had suggested that he should read the autobiography of a young woman, Marie Françoise Thérèse Martin, who had died as a nun in the Carmelite monastery of Lisieux at the early age of twenty-four.

Vernon Johnson was not the first or last to be struck by the simplicity, beauty, depth and love of God which sprang out from the pages of her *Story of a Soul*. Indeed, the Roman Catholic Church had taken the almost unprecedented step of declaring her a saint within less than thirty years of her death.

Of Sister Thérèse during her lifetime, one of the other members of the Carmelite community had said: 'Whatever shall we say about Sister Thérèse when she dies?' Yet, the story she wrote of her life and spiritual journey by order of her superior, which was scribbled on the pages of an exercise book, soon flooded the world and enraptured many millions of hearts. How this all came about, much of it in her own words, is the content of the pages which follow.

But to return for a moment to 1947. Vernon Johnson on being 'captured' by the spiritual doctrine of the saint had gone immediately to Lisieux and had been introduced to her sisters who were still members of the Carmelite community in Lisieux. Getting to know them well, he frequently returned there, and as two of them, Pauline and Céline, remained in the monastery till and beyond 1947, it was through him and his close understanding of both the saint and the recollections of her sisters that I was introduced to the background of her life and the simplicity of her unique contribution to spirituality – the Little Way of Spiritual Childhood.

By remarkable providence, in the devastation of the bombing, the Carmelite monastery, the ancient cathedral church of S. Pierre, the family home of the Martins, Les Buissonnets, and the large modern pilgrimage basilica survived the general destruction.

I was privileged to visit Alençon where the family originally lived and where Thérèse was born, to spend long hours in the Carmelite chapel, to wander through the house and garden of Les Buissonnets, and to stand in the typical French cemetery on the hillside above Lisieux where Thérèse was originally buried. And all this in the company of Vernon Johnson, who had both come so close to the surviving members of the family and also been so deeply involved with Thérèse's Little Way.

At that date, the main source book was the Autobiography, together with insights from within the convent. Since then, there has been much research, the collecting of her letters, the collecting of last testimonies and a host of works, learned and simple, analysing her life and doctrine. She has been pooh-poohed and dismissed by some, received adulation from others.

But through all this there comes the phenomenon of a girl who went behind the convent walls at fifteen and never emerged again, until her body after her death at twenty-four was taken out for burial. Yet she has become and remains an inspiration for millions of twentieth-century Christians and her life is known throughout the world.

These pages seek only to bring again the life, simplicity and love of God from Thérèse of Lisieux to touch a few more hearts. From here, the hope will be that you will be led to study her more deeply, yet still simply, so that the words of Solomon which struck her so fully may apply to each reader: 'Draw me: we will run after you.'

MICHAEL HOLLINGS
The Feast of St Thérèse
1 October 1980

The Martin Home and Family

Louis Martin was born in Bordeaux in 1823, and later moved with his family to live in Alençon in lower Normandy. When he was twenty, he wanted to be a monk and went to the famous monastery of the great St Bernard. But they turned him away.

A short time after this, Zélie Guérin, who also lived in Alençon, went with her mother to seek admission to the convent of the Sisters of Charity. The Sister Superior in interviewing her decided that she did not have a vocation to the religious life, but that God wanted her to live in the world. With humility she returned home and accepted that she was not worthy to be a nun, so she should marry and have children. Her constant prayer after that was 'I beseech Thee to make me the mother of many children, and to grant that all of them may be consecrated to Thee'.

In 1858 Louis and Zélie were married in the church of Notre Dame in Alençon. Altogether they had nine children, seven girls and two boys. Two of the girls and both boys died young. They ardently desired another boy, but the last of their family born on 2 January 1873 was Marie Françoise Thérèse. Two days later she was baptized in the same church of Notre Dame where her parents had been married.

The Martins were a hardworking pair. M. Martin had a jewellery and watchmaking business. His wife, much occupied with the care of her children, supplemented the family income by involving herself in the local industry, making Alençon lace. Each morning, husband and wife went to Mass at 5.30. They were very strict in all their religious observances, prayed together in the home and kept Sunday as a complete day of rest.

Their charity and care for those in need were well known. Their home was open to those in distress and many stories were told of M. Martin's kindness and generosity even in the streets.

But almost immediately, the little Thérèse suffered the first of many partings which were to mark her life. Owing to illness, she had to be placed in the country with a foster mother, and did not return to Alençon for fourteen months. After that, her eldest sister, Marie, was largely responsible for her, a responsibility which was even fuller when the second parting took place. When Thérèse was only four and a half years old, Zélie Martin died after a long and painful illness. But the atmosphere of the home, which can so profoundly influence children, was deeply established. The early memories of Thérèse – she was gifted with strong and clear remembrance back to the age of three – were happy ones.

'My first recollections are of loving smiles and tender caresses; but if God made others love me so much, He made me love them too, for I was of an affectionate nature. You can hardly imagine how much I loved my father and mother, and being very demonstrative, I showed my love in a thousand little ways, though the means I employed make me smile now when I think of them.'

Though Marie was in charge, it was Pauline who was to be the greater influence right through Thérèse's life, even though she was away at school much of that early time: 'I was proud of my two big sisters, and thought of you from morning till night. From the time I began to speak, whenever my mother asked me "What are you thinking about?" my invariable answer was "Pauline". Sometimes I heard them say Pauline would be a nun, and without quite understanding what that meant I used to think: "I will be a nun too." This is one of my earliest recollections and I have never changed my mind; so you see, when I was only two years old, it was your example which drew me.'

The whole family was shattered by the death of the wife and mother. Perhaps M. Martin never completely recovered. It certainly changed Thérèse. Her mother had written to Pauline about her when she was nearly three: 'Baby is the dearest little rogue; she will kiss me and at the same time wish me to die. Oh, how I wish you would die, dear Mother. Astonished at being scolded for saying such a thing she will answer, "It is because I want you to go to heaven, and you say we get there when we die." In her outbursts of affection for her Father, she wishes him also to die.' But writing later in her autobiography to her sister Pauline, who was then Superior of the convent, she says: 'Immediately after Mother's death, my naturally happy disposition deserted me. You know how from being lively and demonstrative, I became timid and shy, and so sensitive that a look was often sufficient to make me burst into tears.'

To bring them near his sister-in-law, M. Martin, who had sold his business some years before, now moved to Lisieux. And so they came to live in a smallish, bourgeois house called Les Buissonnets. Secluded behind high hedges, it had a lawn and flower beds in front and a kitchen garden behind, and it became the scene for the rapid and remarkable spiritual growth of this young girl, through a mixture of happiness, love, trials and a nervous condition lasting until she was fourteen years old.

On the day of their mother's burial, Céline, the sister next in age to Thérèse and whom Thérèse was wont to copy, flung herself into Marie's arms and declared: 'You will be my mother.' Not to be outdone, Thérèse went to her other sister and announced: 'Pauline will be my mother.' Indeed Pauline took on the task of educating her sister with a firm authority and care which drew both happiness and hard work from Thérèse. It was a homely but strict routine, backed by M. Martin, with penalties like missing the afternoon walk if there was not enough work done. Such discipline seems to have been very necessary for the young Thérèse, for her mother had earlier written of her: 'Her stubbornness is almost unconquerable. When she has said "No", nothing will make her change; one could leave her all day in the cellar without getting her to say "Yes"; she would sooner sleep there.'

Without a mother and with Pauline playing that role, Thérèse became more than ever attached to her father. He called her his 'little Queen', and much of her story between the death of her mother and her entry to Carmel centres on her relationship with him: 'Each afternoon I went with him for a walk, and made a visit to the Blessed Sacrament in one or other of the churches. It was in this way that I first saw the chapel of our Carmel: "Look, little Queen," my father said, "behind that grating there are holy nuns who are praying to Almighty God" . . . Those were supremely happy days when my dear "King" as I called him, went fishing and took me with him. Sometimes I tried my hand with a small rod, but more often I preferred to sit on the grass at some little distance. My reflections would then become really deep and without knowing what meditation meant, my soul was absorbed in prayer . . . earth seemed a land of exile and I dreamed of heaven.'

Sunday for her became a highlight in the week, with Mass in S. Pierre. The family sat up near the altar in a side chapel, but at the sermon, M. Martin used to lead Thérèse down to a place in the main body of the church near the pulpit. Later in the day the family would go in turns to their aunt and uncle Guérin, until eventually in the evening they would go home under the stars, Thérèse holding her father's hand and gazing up into the sky where she made out the letter T and would cry out: 'My name is written in heaven.' The evening would end upstairs in Les Buissonnets with night prayers.

It was about this time that Thérèse had a vision in the garden which seemed to foretell another parting in her life. She was looking out of the window filled with happy thoughts. Her father was away. Suddenly she saw a figure dressed like her father, but older and more bent. She could not see his face, because it was covered with a thick veil. She called out in alarm to her father, but the figure continued on and disappeared behind some trees. Her sisters heard her shout, but they could find no explanation. Thérèse never forgot the incident, and later was sure it looked forward to the family tragedy when M. Martin, suffering from frequent paralysis, was affected in his mind, and had to be committed to a mental home.

When Thérèse was eight and a half, Pauline entered Carmel, and hearing she was leaving home, Thérèse was inconsolable. But before entering, Pauline explained the life of a Carmelite to Thérèse, and she thinking it over by herself decided that was where God wanted her too to be. So when the family paid a visit to the Mother Prioress, Thérèse contrived to be alone with her and told her secret of her vocation. The Prioress listened to her, expressed her belief in Thérèse's vocation and at the same time said no one could enter at her age of nine. She must wait until she was sixteen.

Once more the sensitivity of Thérèse was hit hard. She describes the visit she made to Carmel on the day Pauline entered: 'In the afternoon of the same day, October the second, 1882, I saw you behind the parlour grating of Carmel. My dear Pauline was now Sister Agnes of Jesus. How much I suffered in that parlour! It seems to me that because this is the story of my soul, I ought to tell you everything. I must therefore acknowledge that the first pain of our parting was nothing when compared with what followed. I, who had been accustomed to perfect freedom of intercourse with my little mother, heart to heart, could now scarcely snatch two or three minutes with Sister Agnes of Jesus at the end of the family visits. I spent these minutes in tears; then, still in tears, I would come away.'

Resulting from this, and perhaps also from over-rapid development, Thérèse fell ill, with constant headaches, strange shiverings and so on. Her only respite was on the day of Pauline's clothing as a Carmelite, but that itself proved too much for her and she had a serious relapse, and became delirious. At last, M. Martin had a novena of Masses offered at Our Lady of Victories in Paris. During this novena, one Sunday Thérèse began calling out for Marie, and did not recognize her when she entered the bedroom. Unable to do anything, Marie left the room and Thérèse's other sister Léonie picked Thérèse up and took her to the window. Marie was now in the garden, but though she called up to Thérèse, she still did not recognize her. So in tears, Léonie put her back in bed, and together Marie, Léonie and Céline knelt and implored the intercession of Our Lady, whose statue was in the bedroom. Thérèse describes what happened next: 'Suddenly the statue became animated and radiantly beautiful – with a divine beauty that no words of mine can ever convey. The look upon Our Lady's face was unspeakably kind and sweet and compassionate, but what penetrated to the depth

15

of my soul was her gracious smile. Instantly all my pain vanished, my eyes filled, and big tears fell silently, tears of purest heavenly joy.'

This illness and the cure, together with her first Holy Communion for which Marie prepared her and her Confirmation, helped the spiritual growth of Thérèse. Indeed at school the chaplain called her his little 'Doctor of Theology'. She appears, if anything, to have been rather over-serious during this period, and not very good at mixing with her school companions. She had scruples and had to be taken away from school . . . none of this seeming very hopeful for her future. She was sent to a private teacher, and when she went to the convent twice a week to become a member of the Children of Mary, she crept away after the lesson to wait in the chapel till her father came. Tears flowed again when Marie left home for Carmel . . . none of it augured well.

However, at Christmas 1886 there occurred what Thérèse was to call her conversion. She describes it as follows: 'On reaching home after midnight Mass, I knew I should find my shoes in the chimney corner, filled with presents, just as when I was a little child, a fact which proves that I was still treated as a baby. My father loved to watch my enjoyment, and to hear my cries of delight as I drew each new surprise from the magic shoes.' But on this occasion it was different. As she went upstairs she heard her father say: 'All this is far too babyish for a big girl like Thérèse, and I hope this is the last time it will happen.' 'These words cut me to the very heart,' she admitted; and Céline tried to prevent her from going down, for fear she would cry in front of her father . . . But Thérèse was no longer the same – Jesus had transformed her. 'Choking back my tears, I ran down to the dining-room, making every effort to still the throbbing of my heart, I picked up my shoes and gaily drew out the presents one by one, looking all the time as happy as a queen . . .' Céline thought she must be dreaming, but happily it was a sweet reality, and Thérèse had once for all regained her strength of mind which left her when she was four and a half.

From this moment, her vocation developed, a vocation not only to enter Carmel, but to receive the love of God through

Thérèse's father, Louis Martin, and mother, Zélie, née Guérin

Alençon lace, such as Thérèse's mother made

Her father's watchmaker's shop in Lisieux

The Martins' house, 'Les Buissonnets', in Lisieux

Living room at 'Les Buissonnets'

Thérèse aged 8

A drawing of the farmhouse of St Ouen by Thérèse aged 12

Thérèse aged 13

Left Thérèse aged 15

Below Timbered houses in Lisieux

Mother Agnes of Jesus,
elder sister of Thérèse

The Carmelite Church of Lisieux

The garden courtyard
of the Carmelites at
Lisieux

Thérèse in the
Joan of Arc play

the sufferings of Christ, and to pass it on to other souls. The most celebrated example she gives of this is her adoption in prayer of the notorious murderer Pranzini who was condemned to death and was impenitent. Determined to win his repentance, Thérèse asked God to give her a sign that this had happened, even though she said she would accept that he had granted her request even if there was no sign. After his execution she read the account in the newspaper. Having mounted the scaffold without confession, he suddenly turned to the priest, seized the crucifix round his neck and kissed the Christ figure three times. Her vocation to pray for souls was confirmed. She felt herself as pouring out Christ's Precious Blood and took herself more and more to study, mostly through the Imitation of Christ.

At the same time, she grew more determined than ever to enter Carmel. Though she was only fourteen, she plucked up courage to tell her father at the feast of Pentecost, after her Christmas conversion, hoping to be able to enter on the anniversary the following Christmas. They walked and talked in the garden of Les Buissonnets and both wept. Finally, he picked a little white flower from a low wall, saying how God with loving care had preserved it to that day. In doing so he actually pulled it up by the roots: 'It seemed destined to live on, but in other and more fertile soil. My father had just done the same thing for me, by permitting me to leave the sweet valley of my childhood years for the mountain of Carmel.'

There followed a chain of frustration for Thérèse. With her father's consent, she thought she could enter quite simply and immediately. First her uncle objected that she was much too young. This opposition soon melted, but Pauline then told her that the Superior of the Carmel, Canon Delatroette, the local parish priest, would not let anyone enter under the age of twenty-one. A visit to him produced a firm 'No', so next they set off for the Bishop of Bayeux, visiting him at the end of October 1887. The Bishop tried to make Thérèse understand that she should remain at home with her father for some time longer, but her father backed her up. The Bishop then said he must talk to the Superior, and her dream was once more shattered.

Her father then took her on a pilgrimage to Rome, which people thought was an effort on his part to change her ideas about entering religious life. Thérèse comments: 'It might well have injured a vocation less firmly established.' She found her fellow pilgrims people of rank, and was unimpressed. Indeed it led her and Céline to reflect upon the emptiness of earthly titles. She also came closer to priests than she ever had done before and began to understand the chief aim of Carmelite Reform . . . she now knew better that priests were not all good, pure holy men, and that she would have a vocation in life to pray for priests.

If she was not over enthusiastic about her human companions, Thérèse was deeply affected by the places she passed through and visited on her way to Rome. She found her soul lifted up to God by the beauty of Switzerland, and later wrote: 'I understand how easy it would be to become wrapped in self, and to forget the sublime end of one's vocation. Later on, I thought, when the time of trial comes – when I am enclosed in Carmel and shall be able to see only a little space of sky – I will recall this day and it will encourage me. I will make light of my own small troubles by thinking of the greatness and majesty of God; I will give my heart to him alone and avoid the misfortune of attaching myself to fleeting trifles, now that I have glimpsed what is reserved for those who love him.'

In Milan, it was first the cathedral and then the Campo Santo, the cemetery, which impressed her. Venice she found still but melancholy; Padua and Bologna did not seem to make much impression. It was Loreto and the visit to the Holy House which filled her heart with joy. She and Céline were not content as the other pilgrims were with attending Mass in the main basilica, but found their way into the Holy House itself, contained within the main church and reputed, by tradition, to have been carried to the spot by angels. Here they found a priest about to offer Mass, and managed to attach themselves to him and so receive Holy Communion with 'a joy which no words can express'.

So next to Rome, where once more Thérèse and Céline broke away from the rest of the party at the Coliseum, and scrambled down through the rubble to the very floor of the ancient arena, ignoring M. Martin's shouts. Thérèse wrote: 'My heart beat violently when I pressed my lips to the dust once reddened with the blood of the early Christians. And as I begged for the grace to be also a martyr for Jesus, I felt a deep conviction that my prayer was heard.' After the Coliseum, it was the Catacombs and the Church of S. Agnese which most impressed Thérèse, but all the time she was thinking forward to the end of the visit when there was to be an audience with Pope Leo XIII.

The Bishop of Bayeux had remained silent on the question of her vocation. No word had come to Rome, though he had promised that his answer would come while they were in Italy. So Thérèse had determined in her own mind that she would herself ask the Holy Father for his permission. On 20 November all the pilgrims attended the Pope's Mass in his own private chapel, and Thérèse was much encouraged because the Gospel of the day included the words: 'Fear not little flock, for it has pleased your Father to give you a kingdom.' So her heart was filled with confidence as the audience began.

Each pilgrim in turn came to kneel before the Pope, kissing first his foot and then his hand, and finally receiving his blessing. No one said anything, but as Thérèse drew near, the Vicar-General of Bayeux, the Bishop's right-hand man, as though sensing what Thérèse might do, said in a loud voice that he absolutely forbade anyone to address the Holy Father. Thérèse looked to Céline for counsel, and she urged her to speak: 'The next moment I was on my knees before the Pope. After I had kissed his foot he extended his hand, and then, raising my eyes which were blinded with tears, I said imploringly: "Holy Father, I have a great favour to ask you." He at once bent down towards me until his head almost touched my own, while his piercing black eyes seemed to read my very soul. "Holy Father," I repeated, "in honour of your jubilee, allow me to enter Carmel at the age of fifteen."

'Surprised and displeased, the Vicar-General said quickly: "Holy Father, this is a child who desires to become a Carmelite, and the Superiors of the Carmel are looking into the matter." "Well, my child," said His Holiness, "do whatever the

Superiors may decide." Clasping my hands and resting them on his knee, I made one last effort: "Holy Father, if only you were to say 'Yes' everyone else would be willing."

'He looked fixedly at me, and said clearly, each syllable strongly emphasized: "Well, child! well, you will enter if it be God's will." Once again I was going to plead, when two of the noble Guards bade me rise; seeing however that the request was of no avail, and that my hands remained resting on the knees of His Holiness, they took me by the arms, and with the help of the Vicar-General, lifted me to my feet. Just as I was being thus forced to move, the dear Holy Father placed his hand gently on my lips, then, raising it, blessed me while his eyes followed me as I turned away.'

And so, once more, Thérèse for all her determination and boldness seemed to have failed in her request. She gave way to tears and felt a crushing sorrow and failure. But she was consoled by the Pope's last words about the will of God, and she recalled how she had already given herself to Jesus in her simple way as she put it: 'to be his plaything . . . as a little ball of no value that could be thrown on the ground, tossed about, pierced, left in a corner, or pressed to his heart, just as it might please him.' Now she thought of Jesus as having let the ball drop and going to sleep . . . she was desolate, but she continued to hope.

The rest of the pilgrimage took them to Naples, to Assisi, to Florence and then back to France via Pisa and Genoa. Thérèse maintained herself outwardly as before and as though nothing had been said to the Pope. She loved the beauty of the coastal journey back, but was happy once more to be home and to go to visit her sister Pauline, Sister Agnes of Jesus, and to tell her all that had happened. Pauline advised writing a letter to the Bishop of Bayeux reminding him of his promise. This Thérèse did, but Christmas came and went, and there was no answering letter from the Bishop: 'Jesus was still sleeping. He had left his little ball on the ground without even glancing at it.'

Almost immediately after that, however, at the beginning of 1888, the Mother Prioress wrote to Thérèse saying the Bishop had given permission on the feast of the Holy Innocents, 28

December 1887, for Thérèse's immediate entry to Carmel, but that she herself had decided not to open the Carmel doors until after Lent.

Thérèse admits that this sent her into tears once more, and that she was even tempted to throw off restraint and lead a less strict life than usual. However, she resisted this and instead 'I made my mortifications consist simply in checking my self will, keeping back an impatient answer, rendering a small service in a quiet way, and a hundred other similar things. By means of these trifles, I prepared myself to become the spouse of Christ, and I can never tell you, dear Mother, how much the enforced delay helped me to grow in self-abandonment, humility and other virtues.'

The little way of spiritual childhood had begun, though it was not to be defined until considerably later on.

Entering Carmel

So, the moment came for Thérèse to have her heart's desire fulfilled. And it was only natural that the new and longed for parting should be in her own words 'heart-rending', yet at the last moment, when there were sobs all round her, she was dry-eyed: 'I did not shed a tear, but as I led the way to the cloister door the beating of my heart became so violent that I wondered if I was going to die. Oh, the agony of that moment! One must have gone through it to understand it.

'I embraced all my loved ones, then knelt for Father's blessing, and he too knelt as he blessed me through his tears. To see this old man giving his child to God while she was still in the springtime of life was a sight to gladden the angels.'

But once she was inside the enclosure, Thérèse felt not only the warmth of welcome from her sisters, but also from her adopted family of the rest of the community. However, even at this moment she was not to get off entirely without a scar. While the enclosure door was still open and her family standing by, the Ecclesiastical Superior who had all along been against her early entry said in a loud voice to the Mother Prioress: 'I trust she may not disappoint your hopes, but I remind you that, if it should turn out otherwise, the responsibility will be yours alone.'

This did not ruffle the calm of her spirit, and she was truly delighted by the simplicity of the cell to which she was allotted. As she later wrote: 'I was amply rewarded for all I had gone through, and it was with untold joy that I kept repeating: "Now I am here forever".'

It is hard for those of us who have not been through it, to envisage life inside an enclosed convent. The newcomer is chiefly in touch with two sisters – the Mother Prioress and the

Novice Mistress. Thus the attitude that is adopted by these two can be a source of joy or trial to the eager entrant. In Thérèse's case, she was greatly attracted to the Prioress, Mother Marie de Gonzague and also to the Novice Mistress, Mother Marie of the Angels. They were very different characters, but perhaps neither of them fully understood Thérèse's nature. The Mother Prioress from the beginning treated her with severity. Thérèse notes that this was sometimes unconscious on her part, but it is also true that Mother Marie de Gonzague acted on the principle which she declared: 'Dispensations are not for a soul of such metal.' And so it was that she never met Thérèse without finding fault, as for instance when Thérèse was sent out each afternoon into the garden to do some weeding and meeting her, Mother Marie de Gonzague remarked: 'Really, this child does absolutely nothing! What are we to think of a postulant who must be sent out for a walk every day?' Thérèse remarks: 'And this was her invariable method of dealing with me.'

However, hard as it was, and especially the impossibility she found of speaking to the Novice Mistress, Thérèse came to realize how important these trials were, because she knew that she could easily have loved these two in a human way and become over-attached to them. Instead she learned to make an offering of her trials and opened her heart to suffering rather than to affection, thus learning more deeply how she must follow the path of suffering if she was to follow Jesus, and especially to fulfil her intention as she stated it on entering Carmel: 'I have come to save souls and especially to pray for priests.'

Though Thérèse appreciated the Novice Mistress, thought of her as a perfect type of Carmelite and a saint, she did not expand under her guidance, and indeed found the spiritual direction periods with her a real martyrdom. She was helped only in two ways. One of the older former Superiors spoke to her in recreation once, and suggested she had little to say to the Superiors: 'Because your soul is extremely simple. And when you are perfect, you will become more so, for the nearer one approaches to God the simpler one becomes.' Thérèse recognized the truth of this, and though it continued to be a trial that she was unable to open up, it also led her more deeply into simplicity.

The other bonus she had was meeting with Father Pichon, who immediately sensed her quality and gave her great encouragement about her state. She was able to open up to him, but in the way that God so often seems to work, this consolation was removed in yet another parting, for no sooner had she really come to know him than Father Pichon was sent off to Canada. However, before he left, his parting words were: 'My child, may our Saviour always be your Superior and your Novice Master.' So indeed Thérèse turned to the Lord, and from this time on, through the help of Sister Agnes, she came to understand the beauty and meaning of the Holy Face of Jesus, battered and suffering, and she came to wish that: 'Like the face of Jesus, mine should be as it were hidden and despised, so that no one on earth should esteem me: I thirsted to suffer and be forgotten.'

During this period, there was the added trial of a recurrence of her father's paralysis, though he was sufficiently well to take part in her clothing, the first step on her way to religious profession. She was clothed on 10 January 1889, and being a great lover of snow she prayed that it might snow on that day. However it was quite warm, and no one expected that there would be snow, until after the ceremony, they came out into the cloister and found the ground completely white. Thérèse saw it as a delicate gift for her from Jesus. Only a month later, her father was removed from Lisieux and put into a private mental home. For all the family this was a sad blow, but instead of being embittered by it, not only did Léonie and Céline, who were still out in the world, accept it with complete resignation, but Thérèse wrote in hindsight: 'In heaven we shall delight to dwell on those dark days, and even here the three years of our dear Father's martyrdom seem to me the sweetest and most fruitful of our lives. I would not exchange them for the most sublime ecstasies, and in gratitude for such priceless treasure my heart cries out: "Blessed be Thou for the days wherein Thou didst afflict us."

'Dear Mother, how sweet and precious was the bitter chalice, since from each stricken heart there came only sighs of grateful love. We no longer walked – we ran, we flew along the road to perfection.'

This attitude may seem strange to many who would feel at odds with God for allowing such a thing to happen to this good man, who only shortly before had been told by his other daughter Céline that she too wanted to enter Carmel. But Thérèse saw beyond this ordinary feeling of resentment and bitterness. As she said to Céline: 'Far from making any complaint to Our Saviour for the grace he has sent us, I cannot comprehend the infinite love that has urged Him to deal with us in this way. Our Father must be greatly loved by God, since he has so much to suffer. What a delight to share in his humiliation.'

As though this was not enough, Thérèse felt her own spiritual aridity increase and that she could get no comfort from heaven or on earth, and yet she says: 'Amid these waters of tribulation so eagerly thirsted for, I was the happiest of mortals.' Moreover, her next step forward, her profession, which should have taken place at the end of her year as a novice, was expressly forbidden by the Superior of the Carmel, who was still maintaining his original opposition. Thérèse had to wait a further eight months. Instead of turning inwards in resentment, she concluded that her desire for her profession was over-eager and therefore self-indulgent. She set to work to make sure by her simple way of life and her desire for poverty, hiddenness and self-sacrifice that there would be no reason which was her own fault to delay the great day. For her, the important element was to try to accept all that happened. Many of the things would seem very trifling to people in the world, but within the enclosure and founded on an attitude of love and generosity, each little incident had its own particular value. For instance, Thérèse writes of one lesson Jesus taught her: 'One evening, after Compline, I searched in vain for our lamp on the shelves where they are kept. I concluded rightly that a sister had taken it believing it to be her own, and during the time of the "Great Silence" (between Compline and until after Morning Prayer) I could not ask to have it back. Must I then remain in darkness for a whole hour, just when I had counted on doing a great deal of work? Without the interior light of grace I should undoubtedly have pitied myself, but in the midst of the darkness I found my soul divinely illumined. It was brought home to me that poverty consists in being deprived not only of what is convenient but also of what is necessary, so that I felt happy instead of aggrieved.'

On another occasion, what she calls her first victory, she confesses it cost her a great deal: 'It happened that a small jar that had been left by a window was found broken. Believing I was the culprit, our Novice Mistress reproached me for leaving it about, adding that I was most untidy and must be more careful for the future. She seemed displeased, so without saying a word in self-defence I kissed the ground and promised to be more orderly. I was so little advanced in perfection that even trifles like these cost me dear.'

Thérèse is Professed

Despite the delay, the time for Thérèse's profession eventually began to come round, but unlike so many who came to that point with light and enchantment at the signs of the warmth of God's love, she found herself again in darkness. This time it was of an even more difficult kind: In her retreat she describes the situation as one where Jesus led her along an underground path 'where it is neither hot nor cold, where the sun never shines, into which no wind or rain can find an entrance'.

But such was her development that she wrote to her sister: 'I am grateful to Jesus for making me walk in darkness. I am in profound peace. I willingly consent to remain during the whole of my religious life in this sombre tunnel into which he has made me enter, I desire only that my darkness may obtain light for sinners. I am happy, yes, truly happy, in having no consolations. I should feel ashamed if my love resembled that of earthly fiancées who look for presents from the hand of their betrothed, or eagerly watch his face for the loving smile that delights them . . . Jesus! I would love Him, love Him as He has never yet been loved.'

It would seem that Jesus took her at her word, for the night before she was to make her profession she was faced with a sudden temptation. Her vocation appeared to her 'as unreal as a dream'. 'The devil – for it was he – assured me that I was wholly unsuited to the Carmelite life, and that by entering on a way to which I was not called I was deceiving my Superiors. The darkness became so intense that one fact alone stood out clearly – I had no vocation and must return to the world.' But this time she was able to open herself to the Novice Mistress whom she called out of choir, telling her what she felt her state of soul to be. And the Novice Mistress understood her, laughed at her fears and completely reassured her. Nevertheless she went also to the Mother Prioress to tell the same story, and it was she who drove away the last doubt Thérèse had, with the result that the following day, 8 September 1890, Thérèse pronounced her vows, her soul flooded with joy and that peace 'which surpasses all understanding'. Next to her heart she bore a letter which read:

'Oh Jesus, My Divine Spouse, grant that my baptismal robe may never be stained. Take me from this world rather than allow me to stain my soul by committing the least wilful fault. May I never seek or find anything but Thee alone! May all creatures be as nothing to me and I as nothing to them! May no earthly thing disturb my peace.

'Oh Jesus, I ask for peace . . . peace and above all LOVE . . . love without limit. I ask that for Thy sake I may die a martyr – give me martyrdom of soul or body or rather give me both.

'Grant that I may fulfil my promises in all their perfection; that no one may think of me, that I may be forgotten, trodden underfoot as a grain of sand . . .'

She adds that at the end of that day, the feast of the Nativity of Mary, she laid the crown of roses which she had worn for her profession at the feet of Our Lady, without regret: 'I felt that time could never take away my happiness.'

Two weeks later, on 24 September, she received the veil, on a day which was for her veiled in sorrow. Her father was too ill to come. Though she was profoundly at peace, she could not prevent her tears from falling.

A year later, she faced her next retreat, expecting it to be a time of great trial, but instead the priest understood her perfectly, she unburdened herself to him, and as she wrote: 'He launched me full sail upon the ocean of confidence and love which had so long attracted me, but over which I scarcely dared venture. He also told me that my faults did not grieve Almighty God.'

It was soon after this that the foundress of this particular Carmel was dying in the infirmary. Thérèse went to see her, and the old nun, not knowing Thérèse's state at the time, said to her: 'You are always asking me for a spiritual word – today I give

28

you this one: Serve the Lord in peace and joy. Remember that our God is the God of peace.' In fact Thérèse was in deep darkness and even on the verge of sadness. She says she no longer even knew if God loved her ... but these words brought her light and consolation. And when the holy old sister died, Thérèse saw her last tear shining on her eyelash, and approaching her dead body, caught the tear on her handkerchief.

A year later, while Thérèse was sacristan, there was a violent flu epidemic, and a number of the sisters in the convent died, but for Thérèse it was a time of great compensation because she was allowed to receive Holy Communion every day. (It seems strange to us today to think that even nuns in her day were not allowed daily Holy Communion, but that indeed was the ruling of the Church.) It is of interest, and may well be helpful to others to know that Thérèse was not by any means always filled with joy and concentration either at the time of Holy Communion or when meditating. At one point she writes: 'I suppose I ought to be distressed that I so often fall asleep during meditation and thanksgiving after Holy Communion, but I reflect that little children, asleep or awake, are equally dear to their parents; that to perform operations, doctors put their patients to sleep, and finally that: The Lord knows our frame. He remembers we are but dust.' And at another point, she again refers to this difficulty and writes: 'What can I tell you about my thanksgiving after Communion? There is no time when I have less consolation – yet this is not to be wondered at, since it is not for my own satisfaction that I desire to receive Our Lord, but solely to give Him pleasure.'

With all this inner development, Thérèse remained very human. At one point she confesses in her story how she wanted to imitate her sister and both paint and write poems, as well as doing good for those around her. She would not ask for these natural gifts. She went on: 'To the astonishment of the community I succeeded in painting several pictures and in writing some poems, and in doing good to certain souls. And just as Solomon "turning to all the works which his hand had wrought, and to the labours wherein he had laboured in vain,

29

saw in all things vanity and vexation of mind", so experience taught me that the sole happiness of this earth consists in being hidden and remaining in total ignorance of created things. I understood that without love, even the most brilliant deeds count for nothing.'

She also confesses to childish desires like the one of having snow on her clothing, and adds her love for flowers: 'When I made myself a prisoner at the age of fifteen I gave up forever the delight of rambling through meadows bright with the treasures of spring. Yet I never possessed as many flowers as have been mine since I entered Carmel. In the world young men present choice flowers to their betrothed and in like manner Jesus did not forget me. I received for his altar an abundance of all the flowers I loved best . . . '

Then she goes on to tell of the one and dearest desire for which she longed and worked . . . the entry of Céline to Carmel. But she gave this up as a sacrifice, much as she wanted her to enter, and simply left it to God and prayed for her safety in the world. In fact, it was at this time that M. Martin died. Only once had he managed to come to Carmel in his entire illness, and at that time, as he left he pointed upwards, and in a voice choking with tears said: 'In Heaven.' So, now that he was dead, Céline was freed to enter, but as with Thérèse various obstacles seemed to rise against her, including one of the community who strongly opposed her admission. Thérèse put it directly to the Lord in her prayer, linking her desire with the life and suffering of her father. After Holy Communion one day she prayed: 'Thou knowest, dear Jesus, how earnestly I have desired that the trials my dear father endured should serve as his purgatory. I long to learn if my wish has been granted, but I do not ask Thee to speak to me; all I want is a sign. Thou art aware that one of our community is strongly opposed to Céline's entry to Carmel – if she withdraws her opposition, I shall regard it as an answer from Thee, and in this way I shall know if my father went straight to Heaven.'

And the first person she met after making her thanksgiving that morning was the sister who was in opposition, who came up to her with tears in her eyes and expressed a keen desire for

30

Céline's entrance! Almost at once, the Bishop of Bayeux removed his objections, and the way was clear for Céline to join the community of Carmel.

The Story of a Soul

Thérèse Martin entered the Carmel of Lisieux at the age of fifteen and she died in the same Carmel at the age of twenty-four. To all intents and purposes, once she had gone inside the enclosure, she was lost to the world, and was destined to live and die without anyone except the sisters of the community and her own family knowing anything further of her, except when she was allowed to correspond with one or two other people, either by special permission or by command of her Superior.

In fact, with the death of her father and her sisters all leaving the world for the cloister, there were not many other people apart from the Guérin family who remained as relatives for contact in the outer world.

But towards the end of Thérèse's life, in 1895, Mother Agnes of Jesus (Thérèse's sister Pauline) called her aside and showed her a letter from a young seminarian, studying to be a missionary priest. In the letter, to quote Thérèse : 'He said he had been inspired by St Teresa to ask for a sister who would devote herself especially to his salvation, together with that of the souls one day entrusted to him. He promised that when he was ordained he would always remember in the Holy Sacrifice of the Mass the one who would become his sister in Christ. And thus it was that I was chosen to have this future missionary as my brother.'

About a year later, Mother Marie de Gonzague who was once more Prioress added another missionary. Of this event, Thérèse wrote: 'When I represented that, having given all my slender merits to one future apostle, I feared they could not be given to another, you told me that obedience would double their value.' And so Thérèse accepted these two brothers and wrote of her work for them and for the novices (she had been made assistant

32

Thérèse in the Joan of Arc play,
with Sister Geneviève as St Margaret

Thérèse with the statue of the child Jesus, which she painted

The Carmelite dining room at Lisieux

The Carmelite Sisters doing the laundry

The Sisters haymaking

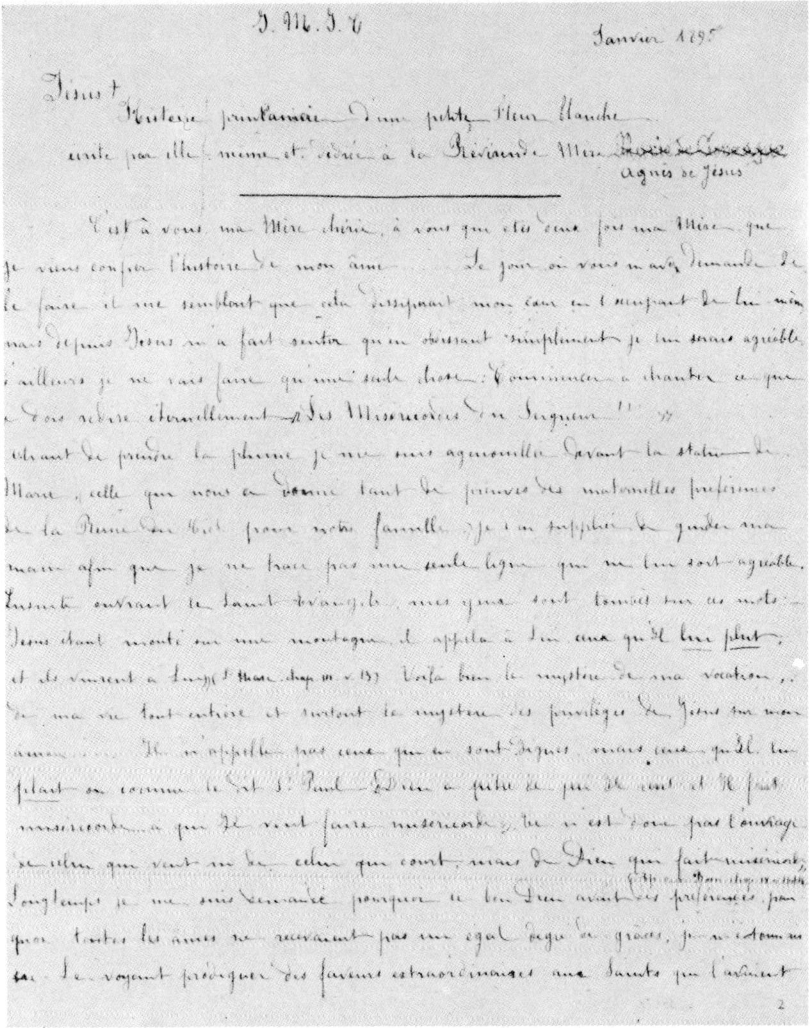

J.M.J.T. Janvier 1895

Jésus †

Histoire printanière d'une petite Fleur blanche

écrite par elle-même et dédiée à la Révérende Mère ~~Marie de Gonzague~~ Agnès de Jésus

C'est à vous, ma Mère chérie, à vous qui êtes deux fois ma Mère, que je viens confier l'histoire de mon âme... Le jour où vous m'avez demandé de le faire, il me semblait que cela dissiperait mon cœur en l'occupant de lui-même, mais depuis Jésus m'a fait sentir qu'en obéissant simplement je lui serais agréable; d'ailleurs je ne vais faire qu'une seule chose: Commencer à chanter ce que je dois redire éternellement "Les Miséricordes du Seigneur!!!"

Avant de prendre la plume je me suis agenouillée devant la statue de Marie, celle qui nous a donné tant de preuves des maternelles préférences de la Reine du Ciel pour notre famille, je l'ai suppliée de guider ma main afin que je ne trace pas une seule ligne qui ne lui soit agréable. Ensuite ouvrant le Saint Évangile, mes yeux sont tombés sur ces mots: "Jésus étant monté sur une montagne, il appela à lui ceux qu'il lui plut, et ils vinrent à lui." (St Marc chap. III v. 13) Voilà bien le mystère de ma vocation, de ma vie tout entière et surtout le mystère des privilèges de Jésus sur mon âme... Il n'appelle pas ceux qui en sont dignes, mais ceux qu'il lui plaît ou comme le dit St Paul: "Dieu a pitié de qui Il veut et Il fait miséricorde à qui Il veut faire miséricorde. Ce n'est donc pas l'ouvrage de celui qui veut ni de celui qui court, mais de Dieu qui fait miséricorde." (Ép. aux Rom. chap. IX v. 15 et 16) Longtemps je me suis demandé pourquoi le bon Dieu avait des préférences, pourquoi toutes les âmes ne recevaient pas un égal degré de grâces, je m'étonnais en le voyant prodiguer des faveurs extraordinaires aux Saints qui l'avaient

2

The first page of Thérèse's *Diary of a Soul*

A picture of Mary Magdelene at the foot of the Cross,
with a handwritten prayer by Thérèse

The chestnut walk in the Carmelite grounds

Thérèse with novices and the Prioress Marie de Gonzague

to the Novice Mistress in Mother Agnes's time as Prioress in February 1893): 'Just as I would have taken a special interest in the work of my own dear brothers if they had lived, without neglecting on that account the general interests of the Church, so now I unite myself in a special manner to the new brothers whom Jesus has given me. To each of them belongs all I possess, for God is too good, too generous to divide my offering: he is so rich that He gives without measure all I ask, even though I do not lose myself in enumerations.

'Since I have two brothers as well as my sisters the novices, the days would be too short to ask in detail for the needs of each soul and I am afraid I might forget something important. Complicated methods are not for simple souls, and as I am one of these, Our Lord himself has inspired me with a very simple way of fulfilling my obligations.

'One day after Holy Communion, He made me understand these words of Solomon: "Draw me; we will run after Thee to the odour of Thy ointments." Oh my Jesus, there is no need then to say: In drawing me, draw all the souls I love. The words "Draw me" suffice.'

So it is that there remain extant in the Carmel of Lisieux various letters from Thérèse to the outside world. Also towards the end of her life, when it was recognized that she could not live long, records of her conversations both with the nuns of the main community and her conversations and work with the novices were preserved.

But the main source and the one which was to touch the people of the world and lead to the canonization of Thérèse was, of course, her autobiography.

In itself, this is a story of the untidy methods of God! Every evening, according to the Carmelite rule, there was a period of recreation for the community, when they sat round together, often doing some sewing or other useful work with their hands, while they chatted to each other. Thérèse describes one of the incidents which occurred and which she turned to spiritual advantage: 'One day during recreation, the portress came to ask for a sister to help her in some particular task which she mentioned. Now I had the eager desire of a child to do this very

33

thing, and as it happened the choice fell on me. I began immediately to fold up our needlework, slowly enough, however, to allow my neighbour to fold hers before me, for I knew it would please her to take my place. Noticing how deliberate I was, the portress said laughingly: "Ah! I thought you would not add this pearl to your crown, you were too slow!" And all the community were left under the impression that I had acted according to nature.'

Anyhow, on one such recreation, Thérèse was entertaining her sisters Marie and Pauline (Sister Marie of the Sacred Heart and Mother Agnes) with some of her recollections of her childhood. Mother Agnes was Prioress at the time, and Marie asked her to realize how valuable what Thérèse had said could be for others and to get her to write down her memories. Mother Agnes was not at first convinced, and took some time to make up her mind. In the end she put Thérèse under obedience to write down her story. This is how Thérèse took the obedience: 'It is to you, dearest Mother, to you who are doubly a mother to me, that I am about to confide the story of my soul. When you asked me to write it I feared the task might unsettle me, but Our Lord has deigned to make me understand that by simple obedience I shall please Him best. I begin therefore to sing what must be my eternal song: "The Mercies of the Lord".'

So it was that this remarkable series of documents began to come into existence. Thérèse could only write during her free time. She was much occupied with the novices, and all the time continued to live in the novitiate rather than in the main community, in humility and to identify with them. She was also the sacristan, which work tended to encroach on her free time. Altogether, the first part which she wrote for Mother Agnes took about a year to complete. It was written in a little exercise book, at the odd moments when she could find time, and during the year of early 1895 to January 1896. One remarkable feature was that there was no crossing out or alteration in the text. This formed the first eight chapters of her autobiography and took her story down to the time of her profession.

One evening when the sisters were assembling in choir for evening prayer, Thérèse came and knelt in front of Mother

Agnes and handed her the exercise book. She simply nodded her head, took the book and put it in her stall, and then did not look at it for several months. It seems she forgot all about it, until she was no longer Prioress, when perhaps she had more time, and read it through. She was struck immediately by the worth of what Thérèse had written, and so went to the then Prioress, Mother Marie de Gonzague, and urged her to get Thérèse to continue her story. It is interesting to note how Thérèse reacted. She made no comment when Mother Agnes had made no mention of the first manuscript for months, showing her self-control and detachment. Now she wrote: 'Dear Reverend Mother, you have expressed the wish that I should finish singing the Mercies of the Lord, and though I will not protest, I cannot help feeling somewhat amused as once again I take up my pen. What I am about to relate you know as well as I do, nevertheless, I obey. I do not even ask what use this manuscript could be, and should you burn it before my eyes without having read it, I should not be in the least distressed.' So were added the next two chapters, nine and ten.

Later again, Thérèse wrote for her sister Marie (Sister Marie of the Sacred Heart) some account of her own special way of life, spirituality and prayer which she referred to as her 'Little Way of Spiritual Childhood'. This forms the final chapter added to the rest of the story of the Mercies of the Lord to make up in a strangely haphazard way a work which has subsequently had a profound effect upon millions of people throughout the world.

During this period of her writing, Thérèse does not seem to have attached much significance to her story, or if she did, her detachment was so great that she could accept that God's purpose for her would be revealed whether what she had written survived or not. But towards the last weeks of her life, she seems to have moved into a realization of the way in which it would be useful for souls well beyond the Carmelite Order. The normal custom in the Order was for a brief summary of the life of any sister who died to be circulated to the other convents. In the case of Thérèse it was decided to send round her own account, and this was very soon not only read with enthusiasm by the sisters, but also passed outside the grille to friends and relatives of the various communities. The first edition came a year after she had died, in 1898, and there were two thousand copies printed, which brought the comment from one of the community: 'Whatever shall we do with these? We shall have them left on our hands!'

As though anticipating this development, Thérèse said on 1 August 1897: 'After my death you must not speak to anyone about my manuscript before it is published. You must speak about it only to Mother Prioress. If you act otherwise, the devil will make use of more than one trap to hinder the work of God, a very important work.' A few days later (4 August) she said: 'No, I don't believe I'm a great saint; I believe I'm a very little soul; but I think God has been pleased to place things in me which will do good to me and others.'

When first published, the manuscript was presented as one whole thing written for Mother Marie de Gonzague. Only later was it made clear that there had in fact been three separate parts, joined together. And later still her letters, poems, last sayings and the depositions from those who knew her, used in the process of her canonization, became public.

What is the 'Little Way'?

The little way of spiritual childhood has already been mentioned more than once in these pages. Perhaps some idea of it may by now have come through the quoted words of Thérèse. But it is time to try to look simply and straightforwardly at the meaning Thérèse gave to the little way, and to some of the development of understanding which has grown since the wider publication of her own writings and the recollections jotted down about her during her last months, together with facts and memories which emerged later.

In writing so far, and in what follows, the aim is to be as simple and little as St Thérèse would have wished. She was insistent and consistent. The little way is ordinary. This was expressed by her firmly to a novice who said on the eve of the feast of Our Lady of Mount Carmel: 'If you were to die tomorrow, after Holy Communion, I think I should be quite consoled – it would be such a beautiful death!' 'Die after Holy Communion!' Thérèse replied quickly, 'upon such a great feast! No, such will never be my lot. Little souls could never imitate me in that. In my "little way" everything is most ordinary, for all I do must be within their reach in the same way.'

The fullest personal explanation given by Thérèse herself was in an exchange with Mother Agnes on 17 July 1897, only two or three months before she died. Mother Agnes had come to see Thérèse in the infirmary, and Thérèse was clearly full of joy: 'Mother,' she said, 'some notes from a distant concert have just reached my ears, and there has come to me the thought that soon I shall be listening to the sweet melodies of Paradise. This thought, however, gave me only a moment's joy, for one hope alone makes my heart beat fast – the love I shall receive and the love I shall be able to give! I feel that my mission is soon to begin

– to make others love God as I love Him . . . to teach souls my *little way* . . .

I WILL SPEND MY HEAVEN
IN DOING GOOD ON EARTH

This is not impossible, for the Angels keep watch over us while they enjoy the beatific vision. No, there cannot be any rest for me till the end of the world – till the Angel shall have said: Time is no more, because the number of the elect will be complete.'

Later she added: 'Would God give me this ever increasing desire to do good on earth after my death unless he wished to fulfil it? No, He would rather give me the longing to take repose in Himself.'

Mother Agnes asked: 'What is the "little way" that you would teach?'

Thérèse answered: 'It is the way of spiritual childhood, the way of trust and absolute self-surrender.

'I want to point out to souls the means I have always found so completely successful, to tell them there is only one thing to do here below – to offer Our Lord the flowers of *little sacrifices* and win Him by our caresses. This is how I have won Him, and that is why I shall be made welcome.'

Earlier on in the section of her story which was addressed to Mother Marie de Gonzague she had written: 'You know I have always longed to be a saint, but in comparing myself with the saints, I have always felt that I am so far removed from them as a grain of sand trampled underfoot by a passer-by is from the mountain whose summit is lost in the clouds.

'Instead of feeling discouraged by such reflections, I came to the conclusion that God would not inspire a wish which could not be realized, and that in spite of my littleness I might aim at being a saint. "It is impossible," I said, "for me to become great, so I must bear with myself and my many imperfections, but I will seek out a means of reaching Heaven by a little way – very short, very straight and entirely new. We live in an age of inventions: there are now lifts which save us the trouble of climbing stairs. I will try to find a lift by which I may be raised to God, for I am too small to climb the steep stairway of perfection."

'I sought to find in Holy Scripture some suggestion of what this desired lift might be, and I came across those words uttered by Eternal Wisdom itself: "Whoever is a little one, let him come to me." I therefore drew near to God, feeling sure I had discovered what I sought. But wishing further to know what He would do with the "little one", I continued my search and this is what I found: "You shall be carried at the breasts and upon the knees: as one whom the mother caresses, so will I comfort you."

'Never have I been consoled by words more tender and more sweet. Oh Jesus! Thy arms, then, are the lift which must raise me to Heaven. To reach Heaven I need not become great; on the contrary I must remain little, I must become even smaller than I am. My God, Thou hast gone beyond my desire and I will sing Thy Mercies.'

We could say that these statements are really the blueprint for the little way. But in addition we can add one more. Thérèse said: 'When I read certain treatises where many obstacles to perfection are shown, my poor mind grows tired very quickly. I close the learned book that wearies my head and dries up my heart, and I take instead the Holy Scripture. Then everything appears to me in a clear light. A single word opens up infinite horizons to my soul. Perfection seems easy to reach. I realize that it is sufficient to recognize one's nothingness and to abandon oneself as a child in the arms of God.'

Without making her simple statements complex, the exposition of her teaching which comes in the remaining pages of this book will try to pick out the main points which she emphasizes and trace them in relation to her own life as she has told us of it, and as others saw her live it. As with the Gospel, it is possible to do all kinds of exegesis and write learned volumes upon her, but she really did intend to teach simplicity, so it would falsify her message if what follows was other than straightforward and as recognizable as possible from her own mouth or pen.

Littleness and Humility in Childhood

Thérèse was the youngest of the Martin family. As such, she remained a child, as she describes herself, almost in a babyish way till she was fourteen, when her Christmas conversion took place. She knew intimately, therefore, from her personal life what it was to live most of her time with those who were older than she. Even when she went to school, she did not find it very easy to mix with her contemporaries.

During much of that time, about five years, she was subject to a strange sadness, sensitivity and easy descent into tears. This in turn gave way to scruples. For many of us, this would seem to be a hopeless kind of start, but part of the wonder of the growth of the young Thérèse was that despite all of these encumbrances, she was still able to have vivid patches of happiness, and also to begin to have insights into the way God was calling her: 'I did not always understand the realities of life,' she wrote of the period before her first Holy Communion and in reference to her reading: 'and in my admiration for the patriotic deeds of the heroines of France, especially the Venerable Joan of Arc, I longed to do what they had done. Then I received what I have always considered one of the greatest graces of my life; for at that age I was not favoured with lights from Heaven as I am now.

'Our Lord made me understand that the only true glory is the glory which lasts for ever; and that to attain it there is no necessity to do brilliant deeds; rather we should hide our good works from the eyes of others, and even from ourselves, so that "the left hand does not know what the right hand is doing". Then as I reflected that I was born for great things, and sought

The four Martin sisters and their cousin Guérin,
as Carmelite Sisters of Lisieux, March 1896

Isidor Guérin, Thérèse's uncle, with his wife, his daughter
Marie and (*right*) his nieces Léonie and Céline Martin

Opposite above The two missionaries, Father
Adolphe Roulland (*left*) and Father Bellière,
with whom Thérèse corresponded
Below Thérèse in July 1896

Thérèse's father confessor,
Father Pichon

The 'oval picture', painted by
Thérèse's sister Céline

Image of the face of Jesus
on the sudarium

Thérèse with her breviary, in which are stuck
pictures of the child Jesus and the image of Jesus
on the sudarium, June 1897

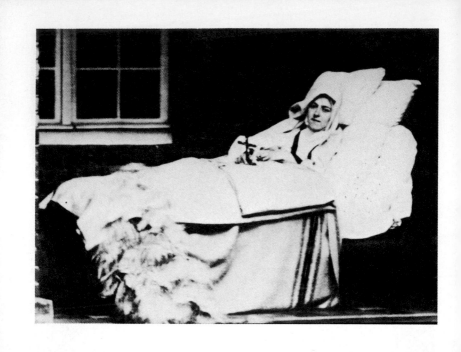

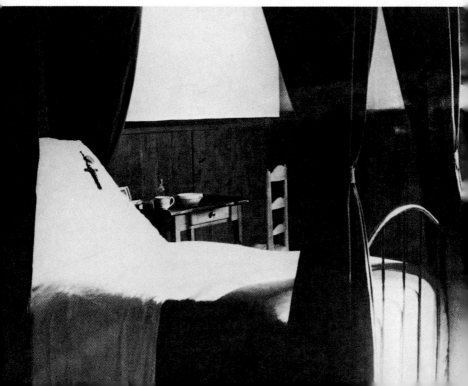

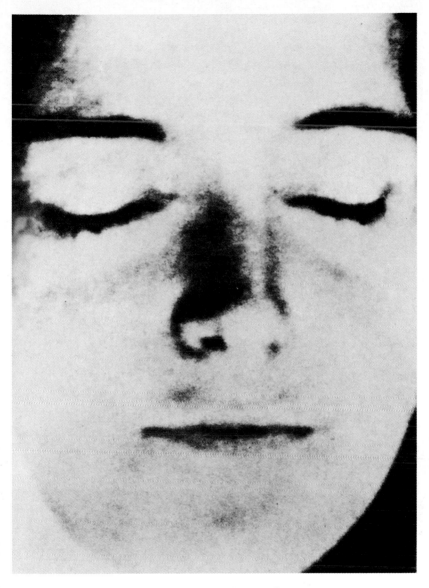

The face of the dead Thérèse, October 1897

Opposite above Thérèse in her sick bed, August 1897
Below The room in which Thérèse died in the Carmelite house of Lisieux

Thérèse with roses. Drawing (1912) by her sister Céline,
Sister Geneviève of the Holy Face

the means to attain them, it was made known to me interiorly that my personal glory would never reveal itself before the eyes of men, but would consist of becoming a saint.

'This aspiration may very well appear rash, seeing how imperfect I was, and am even now, after so many years of religious life; yet I feel the same daring confidence that one day I shall become a great saint. I am not trusting my own merits, for I have none; but I trust in Him who is Virtue and Holiness itself. It is He alone who, pleased with my poor efforts, will raise me to Himself, and by clothing me with His merits make me a saint.'

At that early age, while still in her period of darkness and sensitivity, though she writes about it in hindsight, she is already using in different words the image of the lift.

A little later, she was to receive the Sacrament of Confirmation. Before it Marie helped to prepare her and spoke of suffering. In her simplicity, Thérèse reflected on this and was at the time given to reading the Imitation of Christ. She remarks: 'During my thanksgiving after Holy Communion, I often repeated this passage from the Imitation of Christ: "O my God, Thou art unspeakable sweetness, turn for me into bitterness all the consolations of earth." ' These words, she adds, 'rose to my lips naturally. I said them like a child who, without quite understanding, repeats what a friend may suggest.'

Her simplicity and acceptance of her own powerlessness was already so marked that God would do this in his own way, but as she said somewhere at another stage: 'God only reveals things little by little.'

Looking back, she was quite clear about her weaknesses during this part of her childhood. For instance, when Marie left for Carmel, she recounts: 'I loved her so deeply, I could not bear to be deprived of her gentle companionship.

'I no sooner heard of her determination than I resolved to take no further interest in anything here below, and I shed abundant tears. But tears at that time were nothing unusual; they flowed for the most trivial cause. I was most anxious, for instance, to advance in virtue, yet I went about it in a strange way. I had never been accustomed to wait on myself, or do any housework, and Céline always arranged our room. Now, however, with the intention of pleasing Our Lord, I would sometimes make my bed, or, if Céline happened to be out, I would bring in her plants and cuttings. Since it was for Our Lord's sake that I did these little things I ought not to have looked for any thanks, yet if, unfortunately, Céline did not seem surprised and grateful for my small services, I was disappointed, as my tears soon showed.'

There are two helpful and comforting things which come from that passage. Firstly, Thérèse does not mind admitting her general lack of helpfulness, then her small efforts and then her desire for recognition. This must strike a chord with many ordinary people. We can try to be virtuous, we can even achieve some small services and efforts beyond our normal way of living . . . but how often we really do look for and think we both deserve and need congratulations and thanks for what we have done, even though in theory this was not part of the reason why we decided to do whatever it was. The second point of comfort and help is that Thérèse admits that she openly showed her sister that she was (unjustifiably) hurt, by bursting into tears. It can be that if we are not recognized, we retire into an internal resentment which sours us. Thérèse teaches us that at this stage, openness can be important, as it will later lead us to realize that true littleness is to be hidden.

Perhaps the basic statement on this littleness and humility is in Thérèse's one sentence: 'It seems to me that humility is truth. I don't know whether I am humble, but I know I see the truth in all things.'

For ordinary people like ourselves it is not easy to see ourselves as we are, as we are seen by others, and as we are seen by God. This is a strong reason why each of us needs to follow Jesus out into the desert of prayer, where we can face ourselves and face him, in the somewhat terrifying isolation from the distraction of all those things which can occupy us in our day to day living.

There is also our misunderstanding of God. We spend so much time striving to be better, to achieve, to be something and somebody, to do great things for God. Thérèse reverses the whole of this natural tendency we have. She says: 'It is proper to

42

divine love to lower itself; hence, the lower we are the more we attract God.' In this world of the 'self-made' man, where so much is estimated on success, we are brought back to the phrase of John the Baptist: He must increase, but I must decrease.

Thérèse in her poem 'I thirst for love' puts it this way:

> To ravish Thee, quite little I remain;
> Myself forgetting, I'll charm Thy loving heart.

So complete is the reversal of the common human method and expectation, it is not easy for us to grasp the point.

As G. K. Chesterton wrote in one of his poems:

> The way is all so very straight
> That we may lose the way.

For Thérèse, we must not only recognize our feebleness and incapacity. We must actively love to see ourselves as we really are. She accepts the weaknesses of her nature . . . whether these are pride, selfishness, lack of generosity, fear of pain, sensitivity, or anything else. Like Jesus receiving the Cross, she opens her arms to herself in her nothingness, and expects this to appeal to the merciful love of God.

For you and for me, the lesson is that we readily admit that we are proud, that we have jealousy about other people, we are hurt by lack of recognition, we have strong sexual drives which not only upset us but are even wrongly fulfilled, that we despise others and do them down, that we are thoughtless and less than generous in thinking of the needs of others and trying to supply them. That we are lukewarm in regard to God, his service, praise and love . . . and then by her example, Thérèse says . . . 'Don't go and hide away like Adam and Eve out of fear and loss of face! Come humbly and boldly into God's presence; say: "Here I am. I'm a sinner. Take me! Love me! Save me!"'

But for Thérèse it goes even further than this. If the basic instinct of the modern world is to be recognized and accepted with a status, the basic teaching of Thérèse is to be ignored, forgotten and if thought of, despised.' She went about her daily living in the Carmelite setting, 'rejoicing that she was thought nothing of, forgotten, despised. She accepted the situation of her lover who was 'without beauty, without majesty; no looks to attract our eyes: a thing despised and rejected by men, a man of sorrows and familiar with suffering. A man to make people screen their faces; he was despised and we took no account of Him.' And as a result of this she wanted always to be hidden, unknown and counted as nothing. She puts this in one of her poems, 'I thirst for love':

I want to hide in this world;
I want to be the last of all things,
For you, my Jesus.

Now, this teaching is simple, but for modern men and women, it is not easy. If you are truly going to come to accept this fundamental teaching which she is giving, then it does mean that each of us must give time to be in the desert of prayer. We must face ourselves as we REALLY are. We must then ACCEPT ourselves as we REALLY are, without excuses, but HAPPILY. Then, at that point, God can come down to us, accept us as we really are, and take us on Thérèse's lift of spiritual childhood straight to himself.

'I have many weaknesses,' said Thérèse, 'but I am never astonished because of them. I am not always prompt as I should like to be in rising above the insignificant things of this world. For example, I might be inclined to worry about some silly thing I have said or done. I then recollect myself for a moment and say: "Alas, I am still at the point from which I started." But I say this with great peace and without sadness. It is truly sweet to feel weak and little.'

At this statement, we can feel how far Thérèse has gone both in understanding the everlasting patience of the Lord and in the lesson of accepting herself/ourselves as we are. This reversal of our thought pattern cannot be too fully underlined, because it makes us responsible in the right way . . . responsible for acknowledging our powerlessness, while at the same time recognizing our responsibility for turning to the one source of power in us . . . Jesus. Thérèse wrote: 'We would like never to fall. What an illusion! What does it matter, my Jesus, if I fall at every moment? I come to recognize by it how weak I am, and

44

that is gain for me. You see by that how little I am able to do and You will be more likely to carry me in your arms. If You do not do this, it is because You like to see me prostrate on the ground. Well then, I am not going to worry, but I will always stretch out my arms towards You with great love. I cannot believe that You would abandon me!'

Many of us would feel anxious that we were not, as far as we can judge, advancing in virtue. For anyone who is worried in this way, let us look at ourselves and our personal attitude to failure and lack of advancement in the love of God, so far as we can personally see it. Thérèse was near her death and some kind member of the community brought her something as a gift which might have distracted her from her quietness and recollection. Thérèse refused the gift, because she thought of it as a distraction. But, a few minutes later, she corrects herself and says to the sister who is with her: 'I beg your pardon; I acted on natural impulse.' After a while she added: 'How happy I am to see that I am imperfect and that I am in need of God's mercy, at the hour of my death.'

There is here a simple but deep message, now and at the hour of our death . . . Be simple, be humble, accept God's word . . . Come to me all you who labour and are heavy burdened and I will give you rest!

The Power of Silence

In the noisy world in which we live, where it often seems that the person who shouts loudest receives the most attention, the very silence and hiddenness of God confronts us with a challenge. Indeed, our God is a hidden God.

If one basic foundation for the little way was humility and an acceptance of imperfection and even nothingness, then one of the offshoots of this is necessarily silence.

A person who is humble is probably self-effacing. There is no reason to put 'me' forward. Why should anyone really be interested in me? Why should they want to know about me? What is the point of trying to show off in front of anyone? Why should I try to dominate the conversation?

Thérèse Martin was born of two people who in their own way were silent and humble, to the extent of being very ordinary in an extraordinary way. How many people knew that these two had both wanted to seek God alone in a religious vocation, had been rejected and so had come to married life? How many people knew that they went every morning, rain or shine, to Mass at 5.30 a.m., before they began the work of the day? How many people knew the little acts of charity, the openness of their home to the failures, the distressed and the broken people of the neighbourhood?

M. Martin was a well-to-do bourgeois watchmaker and jeweller. How was he known locally? Did anyone look behind this façade to find the true man who one day at a railway station met a poor and starving epileptic who did not have his fare to get home, so proceeded to take off his hat, and stand begging from the passers-by until he had enough to send the poor man home? – And this but one of innumerable little acts of silent witness to the love of God and love of his poor.

Mme Martin was of the same feeling. Without any show, the housekeeping was ordered so that a system was devised by which a considerable portion of their income went to the work of the Church overseas, and more went to the needs of the local poor. We can hear the future 'littleness and hiddenness' of Thérèse in the words of her mother: 'If they are rich, they desire honours; and if these are obtained, they are still unhappy; for that heart can never be satisfied which seeks anything but God.'

Thérèse herself, though she may well have picked up a great deal from her mother and father, learnt the wonder of silence especially deeply on two occasions which can be pointed out.

When Thérèse has seen the beauty of the Virgin Mary smiling at her as she lay desperately ill in her bed at Les Buissonnets, she recounts her personal feelings: 'The look on Our Lady's face was unspeakably kind and sweet and compassionate, but what penetrated to the very depths of my soul was her gracious smile. Instantly all my pain vanished, my eyes filled and big tears fell silently, tears of purest heavenly joy.

'Our Blessed Lady has come to me, she has smiled on me! How happy I feel! But I shall tell no one, for if I do, my happiness will leave me.' But later she allows Marie to tell the sisters in Carmel of Our Lady's smile, and she goes on: 'All of them as you will remember, dear Mother, questioned me on my miraculous cure. Some asked if Our Lady had the Infant Jesus in her arms; others wished to know if angels were with her. These and further questions troubled and grieved me, and I could only make one answer: Our Lady looked very beautiful; I saw her come towards me and smile.

'Noticing the nuns thought something quite different had happened, I imagined that I had, perhaps, been guilty of an untruth. Had I only kept my secret, my happiness too would have been secure. But Our Lady allowed this trouble to befall me for the good of my soul; without it, vanity might have crept into my heart, whereas now I was humbled and looked on myself with profound contempt. My God, Thou alone knowest all I suffered.'

Her sister Céline (later Sister Geneviève) illustrates her self-control and silence at an early age: 'I was thirteen years old when my father told me that he was going to have me taught drawing. Thérèse was present at the time and I could see her eyes light up with envy, hoping against hope that my father would say that she could learn too. What he said was: "Now, my little Queen, how would you like to have drawing lessons?" She was just going to answer when Marie spoke up and said that the house was already full of "daubs" which needed framing. Marie carried the day. But later, recalling the incident a few weeks before she died, she confessed to me that she felt so violent a desire to expostulate that she still wondered after all those years how she had ever had the strength to resist.'

This self-restraint and understanding of the importance of silence is an aspect we should search out in her own story, because it explains much of the hiddenness of Thérèse and the very ordinariness of her outward life. It could be said of Jesus after his thirty years of hidden life with some astonishment when he begins teaching: Isn't this the son of the carpenter; aren't his brothers and sisters, etc . . . in other words he is so ordinary, what right has he to preach? In much the same way, one of the sisters could say of Thérèse, very near the time of her death: 'Sister Thérèse will soon die and I cannot help asking myself what our Mother will have to say about her after her death, for this little sister, amiable though she is, has surely done nothing worth recording.'

What kind of instances can we give? Her own sister Marie (Sister Marie of the Sacred Heart) was amazed, though she was so close to Thérèse both in and out of the convent: 'It is unusual to see the same invariable equanimity, the same smile forever on someone's lips . . . even during her worst ordeals. Consequently I had no idea how much she was suffering, in her great temptations against faith, for instance, until I read her manuscript after she was dead.'

Here are a few examples . . . there are many more. In the refectory, all the scraps and leftovers were given to her. They used to say in the kitchen: 'No one is going to eat that, let's give it to Sister Thérèse of the Child Jesus. She never refuses anything.'

Thérèse herself recounts a tiresome incident which might

have provoked a reaction from any one of us: 'For a long time at evening meditation, my place used to be in front of a nun who, I think, must have been an exceptional soul – for she hardly ever used a book. That was how I noticed! As soon as this nun came in, she used to begin making a funny little noise which sounded like two shells being rubbed together. I was the only person to notice this, since I have very acute hearing (a bit too acute sometimes). I can't tell you, Mother, how tiresome I found this little noise. I longed to turn round and look at the person who was making it and who was obviously unaware of her mannerism. It was the only way of bringing it to her notice. But deep in my heart I felt it would be better to endure this for love of God and not upset the nun. So I kept still. I tried to unite myself to God and forget the little noise. It was quite useless. I could feel sweat breaking out and was forced merely to make a prayer of suffering, but while I was suffering I tried not to pray in an irritable way, but joyfully and peacefully, at least in my inner soul. Then I did my best to love the horrid little noise. Instead of trying not to hear it – which couldn't be done – I concentrated on listening to it as though it were a magnificent concert, and my entire meditation was spent in offering this concert to Jesus.'

Sister Geneviève again notes an incident towards the end of Thérèse's life: 'At the beginning of her illness, she used to take medicine a few minutes before meals. One old nun was shocked at this and complained on the grounds that it was an infringement of the rule. Sister Thérèse of the Child Jesus would only have to say a word or two to justify herself and pacify the nun in question. She forbore to do so, modelling her conduct on that of the Blessed Virgin who preferred to let herself be defamed rather than justify herself to St Joseph . . . Like Mary's her great method was silence. This was her strength and the basis of her perfection.'

One of her novices recalled asking her a question: 'One day I asked her which was better: to go and rinse things at the cold-water tap or to stay and wash them in hot water in the laundry. She replied: "Oh, that is an easy question! When it costs you an effort to go to the cold tap, that means it costs others an effort too; so go! If, on the other hand, the weather's hot, stay for preference in the laundry. By taking the worst places, you practise self-mortification and at the same time charity for others, since you leave them the better ones." After that, I realized why I used to see her going to the laundry when the weather was hot, and more particularly to the most airless parts of it.'

For Thérèse, as she went on through her life, silence joined her more and more in her hiddenness with Jesus. She was also there in Carmel to pray for the poor, the oppressed, the imprisoned, the voiceless people of the world. Today, when so many feel powerless, so many are deprived of their rights, of their voice, of their human dignity and liberty, Thérèse's silent witness, placing herself utterly in the hand of God, waiting on his mercy, even when he himself is silent . . . all this puts before us an example which is simple, but if lived out, has all the elements of heroism.

Merciful Love and Suffering
in Thérèse's Life

From her early days, Thérèse had an intense desire for sacrifices, mortification and even martyrdom. This grew during her life, coming to a fullness of intention when she made her Act of Oblation as a Victim of God's Merciful Love on the Feast of the Holy Trinity, 9 June 1895. One section of it reads: 'In order that my life may be one act of perfect love, I offer myself as a holocaust to Thy merciful love, imploring Thee to consume me unceasingly, and to allow the floods of infinite tenderness gathered up in Thee to overflow into my soul, that I may become a martyr of Thy love, O my God! May this martyrdom one day release me from my earthly prison, after having prepared me to appear before Thee, and may my soul take its flight − without delay − into the eternal embrace of Thy Merciful Love.

'O my beloved, I desire at every beat of my heart to renew this oblation an infinite number of times, "till the shadows retire" and everlastingly I can tell Thee my love face to face.'

When she was about three years old, the encouragement she had within the family laid the foundation for what was to grow into a loving abandonment to God's love. Her mother wrote in 1876: 'Even Thérèse is anxious to practise mortification. Marie has given her little sisters a string of beads on purpose to count their acts of self-denial, and they have really spiritual, but very amusing conversations together . . . but it is still more amusing to see Thérèse continually putting her hand in her pocket and pulling a bead along the string for every little sacrifice.'

At this stage of her life, Thérèse was not a person to do things

51

by halves. She herself gives us an example: 'Under the impression, no doubt, that she was too big to play with dolls, Léonie one day brought us a basket filled with their frocks and other trifles. On these she laid her doll. "Here, dears," she said, "choose whatever you like." Céline looked at it and took a woollen ball. After a moment's thought I put out my hand, saying: "I choose everything", and I carried off both doll and basket without more ado.

'This childish incident sums up, so to speak, the whole of my life. Later on, when the way of perfection was opened out before me, I realized that to become a saint one must suffer much, one must always choose the most perfect path. I understood that there are many degrees of holiness, each soul being free to respond to the calls of Our Lord, and to do much or little for his love – in a word, to select amongst the sacrifices He asks. Then also, as in the days of my childhood, I cried out: "My God, I choose everything – I will not be a saint by halves, I am not afraid of suffering for Thee. One thing only do I fear, and that is to follow my own will. Accept then the offering I make of it, I choose *all* that Thou willest." '

The encouraging thing about Thérèse is this. When we read the oblation and statements like the one above, we may easily be put off, feel that to speak of 'a little way of spiritual childhood' is really a misstatement, because she seems to make demands upon herself which would be well beyond our capabilities and are far from ordinary. But, if we follow the course of her life, we find that she does not go in for inflicting pain on herself, she does not undertake anything which is unusual in her chosen way of life. Her significance is that she leaves herself open to what comes. She abandons herself to the merciful Love of God, seeing in what happens that Love coming into her life. The difference is that she is content to accept that things of joy or sorrow and of pain are all from God's hand. She does not expect the sun always to be shining, so that when the dark clouds of depression, of family separation, of the sickness and death of her mother and father enter her life, she suffers intensely, but without losing her interior calm and acceptance.

She refers to herself as Jesus's plaything. She is prepared for

Jesus to 'sleep in her boat'. And so she finds in the course of any ordinary day many opportunities for offering small moods, irritations, and the very strictness of the Carmelite rule as little gestures of love to God. For instance, the Martin sisters were a very close family, and it might have been that to have them all in the one convent would have been a source of some relaxing of the rule of silence. However, though it often caused her literally to hang on to the bannisters to get herself past her sister's cell without speaking, Thérèse used the silence as a weapon of love. She was appointed assistant to Pauline (Sister Agnes) soon after she entered, but she was forbidden by the rule to speak unnecessarily. She never allowed herself any word of personal confidences, and even when Sister Agnes became Prioress, and speaking to her was allowed, Thérèse saw less of her than any other of the sisters. They were allowed to talk at recreation, but Thérèse's general practice was not to sit with her sisters, but rather beside sisters whom she found least agreeable. She confessed later to Mother Agnes: 'O my dear Mother, how much I suffered then! . . . I could not open my heart to you and I thought you no longer knew me!'

Thérèse knew well the story of Joan of Arc. She wrote a play about her and acted in it while in Carmel. She knew of her rejection, her questioning, the test of her faith. She relied much on the works of St John of the Cross. She knew of his rejection, his imprisonment, and the misunderstanding surrounding him. She once said to Mother Agnes, when they were talking about hidden virtue: 'That is what struck me about the life of our Father St John of the Cross, when they used to say: "Brother John of the Cross? Why, he's a less than ordinary religious!"' But above all she looked to Mary, Joseph and Jesus for the hidden suffering and complete underlying trust and hope which came through their lives.

For Thérèse, one of the constant sufferings which she bore in the convent life was that of cold. Mother Agnes spoke of this after her death: 'We only realized towards the end of her life that the cold – no doubt owing to her state of health – was particularly a painful ordeal for her. However, she never was seen to rub her hands in winter or adopt an attitude giving the least hint of her suffering. She never said "It's very cold" or "It's hot". She never complained about anything.'

But as her life came towards its close, she was more and more in the hands of God, abandoned to the illness she was suffering, and also both submitting to the horrifying methods of cure attempted by the doctors, and to the simultaneous darkness of faith.

In the book of her last conversations, there is ample testimony of the physical and spiritual suffering that Thérèse had to endure during the last months of her life. Without spreading out the details, suffice it to say that the remedies offered by the doctors were a form of blistering round the chest, poultices deliberately put on to cause blistering, so that these could be burst, in the hope of relieving the chest. There was also a method of pricking in as much as five hundred different spots at a time. To this was added the natural difficulty of thirst, difficulty in breathing, and, for Thérèse, gangrene of her intestines. Nor was death rapid. They thought she would die in July and she lingered on in consciousness and suffering till the end of September.

But we should look at some of the ways in which she very simply lived out the suffering with patience and a sense of humour. The infirmarian advised her to take a little walk each day, and she accepted this under obedience. But one day another sister saw her difficulty in walking and said: 'Sister Thérèse, you would do much better to take a rest; walking can do you no good when you are suffering so much, you are only tiring yourself.' 'That is quite true,' said Thérèse, 'but do you know what gives me strength? I offer each step for some missionary, thinking that somewhere far away, one of them is worn out by his apostolic labours, and to lessen his fatigue I offer mine to God.'

On the whole, she was so smiling and so composed no one realized the extent to which she was suffering. Someone once said to her: 'They say that you have never suffered much.' With a smile she pointed to a glass in which there was some medicine of a bright red colour. 'Do you see this little glass?' she said. 'One would suppose it contained a most delicious draught, whereas in reality it is more bitter than anything I take. Well, it is the image of my life. To others it has been all rose-coloured; they imagine I have drunk the most delicious wine, but to me it has been full of bitterness. I say bitterness yet, after all, my life has not been sad, because I have learned to find joy and sweetness in all that is bitter.' 'You are suffering just now, are you not?' 'Yes,' she answered, 'but I have longed so much to suffer.'

She recognized in herself how far she had come. The novices asked her: 'How do you manage not to give way to discouragement when you are forsaken in this way?' (Thérèse had just asked them to pray for her saying 'often when I cry to heaven for help, it is then I feel most abandoned') She replied: 'I turn to God and to all His Saints and I thank them just the same; I believe they want to see how far I trust them. But the words of Job have not entered my heart in vain: "Even if God should kill me, I would still trust in Him." I admit it has taken a long time to arrive at this degree of self-abandonment; but I have reached it now, and it is Our Lord Himself who has brought me there.'

Much earlier when she was still able to move about freely, she gives another example of her self-abandonment, her detachment. 'One Sunday,' Thérèse said, 'I was going towards the chestnut avenue, my heart filled with glad expectation, for it was spring time and I wanted to enjoy the beauties of nature. What a bitter disappointment: My dear chestnuts had been pruned, and the branches already covered with buds, now lay on the ground. On seeing this havoc, and thinking that three years must elapse before it could be repaired, my heart felt very sore. But the grief did not last long. "If I were in another convent," I reflected, "what would it matter to me if the chestnut trees of the Carmel at Lisieux were cut down to the root? I will not worry about things that pass. God will be my all. I will take my walks in the wooded groves of His love, whereon no one dares lay a hand." '

One of the most lovely revelations of the patience, humour and charity of Thérèse comes at the time in mid-June when she is clear that she cannot be cured. She is pushed out into the convent garden in an invalid chair (incidentally, the one used previously by her father before his death). She has been told to continue the story of her soul. She is full of fever and exhaustion. And this is what she says of the experience: 'Sometimes I would be writing about charity and very often someone would come and interrupt me; then I would try not to be impatient, and to practise what I was writing. As soon as I take up my pen, along comes one of the nuns with her fork on her shoulder. She thinks it will amuse me if she has a little chat. Hay, ducks, chickens, the Doctor's visit; all is grist to the mill. Admittedly this doesn't last long, but there's more than one charitable nun and suddenly another hay-maker lays a few flowers in my lap, possibly thinking to inspire me with poetic thoughts. But poetic thoughts are not what I'm wanting just now and I should have preferred the flowers to stay swaying on their stalks. Eventually, tired of opening and shutting my wretched exercise-book, I open another book (which won't stay open) and say resolutely that I am copying out thoughts from the Psalms and Gospel for our Superior's birthday. And this is true enough, since I don't stint the quotations ... Beloved Mother, I'm sure I should make you laugh if I told you all my adventures in the grove of Carmel. I doubt if I can have written ten lines without being interrupted. This would normally have made me laugh or even amused me, but for love of God and my sisters (who are so kind to me) I try to look happy and above all to be so ... There; you see! there goes another hay-maker, who has just said: "Poor little sister, you must find it tiring writing all day like that." "Don't worry," I said, "I look as if I'm writing a lot, but really I've hardly written a thing." "Oh, good," she said, looking reassured, "but all the same, I'm very glad we're haymaking. It makes a little bit of distraction for you." The fact is, it's a very big distraction indeed.'

There is, however, another side to her suffering and her complete, trustful acceptance which must be looked at, if we are to get the measure of her trial and her generous commitment in faith and trust that the 'Mercies of the Lord' which she is singing will never fail her.

This particular aspect is one which will touch modern man very closely. If we are prepared to listen to her and to learn from her, then there is a simple but profound lesson for this unbelieving world of today.

The area we can now deal with is the area of faith.

It would surely seem to the outsider who has read this far, that here is an exceptional person, who is unlikely to be like ourselves, and especially must be someone who is so strong in faith that nothing will ever shake it, and she must always be lightened with some inner awareness and consolation which carries her through warmly and with assurance. It is just this misconception which we should face as we listen to her experience, and then perhaps we shall find an additional hope and trust ourselves in our personal difficulties and darkness which may invade our lives.

At various times during her life both in and out of Carmel, Thérèse had periods of darkness. We have already adverted to her early scruples and to the long years before her Christmas conversion when she was over-sensitive and readily given to tears. But, for instance, before receiving the habit, she writes to Sister Agnes: 'Dryness and drowsiness – such is the state of my soul in its intercourse with Jesus! But since my Beloved wishes to sleep, I shall not prevent Him.'

Again she writes to Sister Agnes during her retreat before her profession: 'My Spouse speaks not a word, and I say nothing save I love Him more than myself; and in the depth of my heart I know this is true, for I am more His than mine. I cannot see that we are advancing towards our journey's goal, since we travel underground; and yet, without knowing how, it seems to me we are nearing the summit of the mountain.

'I give thanks to Jesus for making me walk in darkness, in the darkness I enjoy profound peace. Indeed, I consent to remain through all my religious life in the gloomy passage into which he has led me. I desire only that my darkness may obtain light for sinners. I am content, no, I am full of joy, to be without consolation.'

This is at the outset of her religious life. She grows, as we have seen, constantly during the years in Carmel. It is only natural then that as that life itself develops, the testing and the severity should also increase. We might well feel that the reverse should be the case. That would be for us to misunderstand the call of Jesus who has asked us to deny ourselves, to take up the Cross daily and to follow him. The example of Thérèse, of her daily taking up the Cross, and of her unwearied continuing even through despair is to be for us a source of strength when we are weak, a source of hope when we are in despair, and a guide to the meaning of love at the point when we want to turn back upon ourselves and to claim that it is all too much, that we cannot go on, and that we deserve a break from darkness.

There are many other possible insights that could be given of the darkness which was present in the austerity of the convent, the misunderstanding of the other sisters, in the severity of the Superiors, in the external pressure of her father's sickness and death, or the possible loss of her sisters to other Carmels in missionary countries. She also had to face hard decisions, like the one when she considered that one sister was becoming too fond of the Prioress, and felt she must tell her. Sister Agnes warned her when Thérèse confided the problem, that if she did so, she, Thérèse, might be sent away. Thérèse accepted the possibility, and still knew she must go ahead with her duty.

But, the greatest trial was not one which came from within the Carmel. It was one for Thérèse herself and for her relationship with the Lord. It came to a full measure during her last illness. One such incident is worth noting. She said to Mother Agnes: 'Last night I was seized with a terrible feeling of anguish. I was lost in darkness, from out of which came an accursed voice: "Are you sure God loves you? Has he come to tell you so Himself? The opinion of a few creatures will not justify you in His sight." These thoughts had long tortured me, dear Mother, when your little note came like a message from Heaven. You recalled the special graces Jesus lavished on me, and, as though you had given me a revelation concerning my trial, you told me I was dearly loved by God, and was on the eve of receiving from His hand my eternal crown. Peace and calm revived my soul. Then the thought occurred that it was perhaps your affection which prompted you to write in this way. Immediately, I was inspired to take up the Gospels, and opening the book at random, I came upon the passage which had escaped me till that time: "He whom God has sent, speaks the words of God, for God does not give the Spirit by measure." '

But this was still not the ultimate trial. On 7 June 1897, very shortly before she learnt for certain that her death was near, Thérèse posed on her knees in the cloister of Carmel for the last time, and she was holding two pictures which sum up her life of littleness and abandonment to the merciful love of God – pictures of the Child Jesus and the Holy Face. She had come to know in her own littleness with the Holy Child that the Face of the love of God – the Merciful Love – was the battered and beaten face of Jesus as it appears on the Shroud of Turin – the face of love.

But for Thérèse to come to know fully what this love meant, she had to go with Jesus through the Agony of the Garden which came to a sweat of blood, and also through the desolation of the Cross, when everything and everybody seemed to have disappeared, including God . . . with Jesus, her beloved, she had to echo: 'My God, my God, why have you forsaken me' . . . and yet be prepared with Jesus to go ahead in utter trust to say: 'Into your hands I commend my Spirit.'

We can see this being lived out in Thérèse as we watch her and listen to her: 'Press on, press on, looking forward to death! But it won't give you what you hope – only deeper darkness still, the darkness of extinction.' So Thérèse wrote on 9 June 1897 and she added: 'I shan't write any more or I might be blaspheming. I fear I have said too much already.'

The simple and important lesson each of us must learn from this suicidal impulse lived through by Thérèse is that she not only said and wrote words implying the suffering which was to come and the almost insufferable desolation, but she was able to bear witness to the truth of what she had foreseen. Look at these indications written to her sister Marie (Sister Marie of the Sacred Heart) a year before she died, in September 1896 . . . but read in relation to the passage quoted above . . . 'Press on' . . .

'How can you ask me if it is possible for you to love God as I love Him! My desire for martyrdom is nothing; it is not to such desires I owe the boundless confidence that fills my heart. They

59

might be described as spiritual riches, which are the "mammon of iniquity", when one takes delight in them as something great . . . these aspirations are a consolation Jesus sometimes grants to weak souls like mine – and there are many such. But when he withholds this consolation, it is a special grace. Remember these words of a holy monk: "The martyrs suffered with joy, and the King of martyrs in sorrow" . . . Did not Jesus cry out, "My Father, remove this chalice from me." Do not think then that my desires are a proof of my love. Indeed, I know well that it is certainly not because of them that God takes pleasure in my soul. What does please Him is to find me loving my little-ness, my poverty, and to see the blind trust which I have in His mercy . . .

'Are you not ready to suffer all that God wills? Assuredly! And so if you wish to know joy and to love suffering, you are really seeking your own consolation, because once we love, all suffering disappears . . .

'Do you not understand that the more weak and wretched we are, the better material we make for His consuming and transfiguring fire? . . . The simple desire to be a victim suffices, but we must also consent to remain always poor and helpless, and here lies the difficulty: "Where shall we find one that is truly poor in spirit? We must seek him afar off", says the author of the Imitation. He does not say we must search among great souls, but "afar off" – that is to say, in abasement and nothingness. Let us remain far from all that dazzles, loving our littleness and content to have no joy. Then we shall be truly poor in spirit, and Jesus will come to seek us, however far off we may be, and transform us into flames of love . . . Confidence alone must lead us to love.'

And part of the utter trust was having to live not only in physical pain but in the accompanying 'far offness' of loss of vision: It is told how one day she was looking at the beauty of the sky, and someone said to her: 'Your home will soon be there, beyond the blue sky. How lovingly you look at it.' She only smiled, but later she said to Mother Agnes, 'O Mother, the sisters do not realize my sufferings. Just now when I was looking at the sky, I was merely admiring the beauty of the material heaven - the real Heaven seems more than ever closed against me.'

That is the lesson we need to take to ourselves. To suffer means to suffer, not to have it relieved. But in the words of Jesus 'your sorrow will be turned into joy'.

The confidence, hope, trust and love of Thérèse move through the sense of being abandoned and the desolation of despair, not cushioning the experience but showing in her experience the meaning of St Paul's words: 'When I am weak, then I am strong.'

Oh, I Love Him

Earlier in her life, Thérèse, within Carmel, was at a loss about her true vocation. She read chapters 12 and 13 of St Paul's First Letter to the Corinthians. She still was not satisfied. From St John of the Cross she draws the phrase: 'Then descending into the depths of my nothingness, I was so lifted up that I reached my aim.'

She continued her meditation on St Paul and afterwards wrote: 'I understand that since the Church is a body composed of different members, she could not lack the most necessary and most nobly endowed of all the bodily organs. I understood, therefore, that the Church has a *heart* – a heart on fire with love. I saw too that love alone imparts life to all the members so that should love ever fail, apostles would no longer preach the Gospel and martyrs would refuse to shed their blood. Finally I realized that love includes every vocation, that love is all things, that love is eternal, reaching down through the ages and stretching to the uttermost limits of earth.

'Beside myself with joy, I cried out: "O Jesus, my love, my vocation is found at last – *my vocation is love*. I have found my place in the bosom of the Church, and this place, O my God, Thou hast given me: in the Heart of the Church, my Mother, *I will be love*" . . . Thus I shall be all things, and my dream will be fulfilled . . .

'I am but a weak and helpless child, but my very weakness makes me dare to offer myself, O Jesus, as victim of Thy love . . . now the law of fear has given way to the law of love, I have been chosen, though a weak and imperfect creature, as Love's victim. And is not the choice a fitting one? Most surely, for in order that Love may be wholly satisfied, it must stoop even into nothingness and transform that nothingness into fire.

' "Love is repaid by Love alone." Well do I know it, my God! And therefore I have sought and have found a way to ease my heart by giving Thee love for love.'

At the very end, she lives this out, in an ordinary and yet extraordinary suffering mixed with joy. Throughout her life, one of the words used frequently by Thérèse has been happiness or joy. She has known plenty of darkness, of sorrow, of physical hardship and spiritual dryness. But all the way through there has been peace, happiness and joy based on the foundation of her utter trust in the Merciful Love of God.

Now, in her final agony she exclaimed: 'Mother, the chalice is full to overflowing! I could never have believed it possible to suffer so intensely and can explain it only by my great longing to save souls . . . My God, whatever Thou wilt, but have pity on me. Sweet Virgin Mary come to my aid . . . All that I have written of my thirst for suffering is really true. I have no regret for having surrendered myself to Love.'

And so, finally, looking at her crucifix her last words are . . . 'O! . . . I love Him . . . My God, I . . . love . . . Thee.'

Thérèse died on the evening of 30 September 1897. On 4 October 1897, the Carmel doors were opened, and her body was taken up the hillside to the cemetery of Lisieux, because the sisters were no longer allowed to bury the community within the convent walls. Léonie alone of the sisters accompanied the coffin, for in 1895 she had left the convent of the Visitation at Caen which she had previously entered in 1893.

Thérèse thus ended the partings which marked the course of her life with her body leaving the enclosure of Carmel. But this, in hindsight, all seems to have been part of the bigger plan of merciful love. The poor plot, the humble grave, the little band of relatives and friends who came away on 4 October 1897 was transformed into a crowd of fifty thousand when the coffin was exhumed on 26 March 1923.

By this time, the prophecy of Thérèse was being fulfilled: 'I feel my mission is soon to begin . . . to make others love God as I have loved Him . . . to teach souls my *little way* . . . I WILL SPEND MY HEAVEN IN DOING GOOD ON EARTH.'